MARYLAND

MARYLAND

PHOTOGRAPHY BY STEVE UZZELL

TEXT BY CARL BODE

GRAPHIC ARTS CENTER PUBLISHING COMPANY
PORTLAND, OREGON

DEDICATION

To My Family
Steve Uzzell

Page 2: Though a Maryland planter in colonial days would never walk when he could ride, his horse meant more to him than mere transportation. Even today the horse occupies a revered status, enjoying lush pastures and racing famous tracks throughout the state. Horses graze north of Baltimore at Sagamore Farm, home of Native Dancer, the winner of the 1953 Kentucky Derby.

Page 5: Near the Aberdeen Proving Ground a tug pulls a barge through the half-frozen Chesapeake Bay. The Bay's numerous arms and inlets give Maryland all but thirty-one of her more than 5,000 mile shoreline.

Small photos, text section. Page 18: Solar breeder, The Solarex Corporation, Frederick. *Page 19, left:* Statue, Antietam Battlefield, *right:* State flag above lacrosse players, University of Maryland, College Park. *Page 22:* Wilde Lake, Columbia, *Page 23, left:* Civil War period photographer near Burkittsville, *center:* Mother and daughter boating off Deal Island, *right:* Balloon race, Sandy Point State Park. *Page 27, left:* Ethnic dancers, Baltimore's Inner Harbor, *center:* Cannon, Antietam Battlefield, *right:* Musket fire, Fort Frederick. *Page 30:* Phoebe in tree, St. Marys County. *Page 31, left:* Carroll County Farm Museum. *right:* Sales identification tag, tobacco auction, Marlboro.

Below: Constantly reshaped by the Atlantic Ocean, Assateague, Maryland's barrier island, conveys a restless mood and beckons all its visitors to explore and discover: A trio of canoeists return after a day of fishing and crabbing. *Left:* A cumulus cloud towers in the amethyst sky above an isolated farmhouse in Queen Anne's County. *Overleaf:* Savoring the season as long as possible: On the last weekend in October, expert crews coax every knot from a pair of ocean racers south of Annapolis in the Skipper's Race, the last big boat race of the season.

Below: A gracious home stands on a rise, commanding a panoramic view of western Montgomery County. *Right:* The handsome double wooden dome, designed by Joseph Clark and completed two centuries ago, rests atop the Maryland State House in Annapolis. Constructed of cypress beams and assembled with wood pegs, it is the largest wooden dome in the United States; the State House is the oldest state capitol in continuous legislative use and the only state house ever to have served as the nation's capitol.

Below: An equine receptionist greets one of the younger of the 20,000 spectators at the Maryland Hunt Cup Race, generally acknowledged to be the world's most difficult timber steeplechase race. First run in 1894, the race has been held since 1922 at Snow Hill in Baltimore County's Worthington Valley. *Left:* A tree-lined Montgomery County drive tries hard in a losing battle to keep its autumn colors.

Below: Promoted in the 1850s as the "Switzerland of America," Garrett County, westernmost in the state, receives almost nine times the snowfall of the Eastern Shore. *Right:* Maryland shows off its earth colors. This rich fall palette is in Allegany County. *Overleaf:* Form and function: Canada geese over the Blackwater National Wildlife Refuge in Dorchester County. Their "V" formation allows all but the leader to fly in favorable air currents. Older, stronger geese alternate the lead.

Sunsets. They're intended to entrance us. The loveliest one I remember at Assateague Island had long bars of carmine light against an aquamarine sky. My favorite in Garrett County, at the other end of the state, was a crimson cone of light between two slate-blue mountains. Of course there's more to Maryland than sunsets. A mundane Maryland exists, with its inevitable deficiencies and difficulties, and it will have to be touched on from time to time in the text. But basically this book is a celebration of the beauty and vitality to be found throughout the state. Steve Uzzell has caught the essence of that beauty in his photographs; and in my introduction I've tried, in the course of surveying the state, to give a sense of that vitality.

* * *

The lay of the land is famous: It's been hailed as "America in Miniature." The state geologist tells us that "America in Miniature" is slowly, very slowly, sinking beneath the sea; its richly variegated surface is giving way to water. But we don't have to worry. It'll need a million years, give or take a hundred thousand, for the ocean to rise high enough to reach from Assateague to Backbone Mountain in Garrett County. Yet the ocean's power is already attested by the three ancient rivers, one drowned and the other two drowning, that interlace the land in the eastern half of the state. Originally Chesapeake Bay was an extension of the Susquehanna River; today it's the Atlantic's largest inlet on the East Coast. The Potomac and the Patuxent are being overwhelmed also, starting with their estuaries.

Meanwhile, the land above the water is divided into three different and noteworthy zones. The biggest is the Coastal Plain, occupying more than half of Maryland and stretching westward from the ocean's edge to the fall line. The fall line, where the hard rock of Appalachia meets the softer stone of the Coastal Plain, runs roughly parallel to the coast, from Washington to Baltimore to Elkton in the northeast corner of the state. The next zone is the Piedmont Plateau, whose pleasant terrain covers the middle of the state, from the fall line to the rim of the Appalachians. It's Maryland's heart-land. Last is the Appalachian area itself, which ends with Garrett County and abuts the mountains of West Virginia and Pennsylvania.

One more zone, important if anomalous, demands to be included. It's Chesapeake Bay. Once the most abundant source of seafood in the country, it still supplies many a dinner table. It also remains a broad highway for transportation. And it's a marvelous place to play, a source of recreation for all sorts of sailors in all sorts of pleasure-boats. Any way we look at it, there's nothing negligible about the Chesapeake. It's close to 200 miles long and covers an area within Maryland of more than 1,700 square miles.

Early in Maryland's history each zone developed a characteristic way of life. Making a living came first, though there was of course much more to the way of life than that. To put it simply, the people of the Coastal Plain supported themselves, generation after generation, by growing tobacco and harvesting seafood; the people of the Piedmont earned their money by producing bumper crops of grain; and the people of Appalachia did mining and logging. Naturally, in Maryland's complex economy, changes were always taking place to a greater or lesser extent and for better or worse. However, they accelerated in several parts of the state with the coming of the twentieth century. The reasons could be found in a variety of circumstances ranging from the advent of the automobile to the exploitation of both land and water. The changes were social as well as economic.

We might describe the general situation briefly, not only for its own sake but because it shows something about human nature— especially on the two sides of the Chesapeake. To take the Coastal Plain first then, we see that the Chesapeake splits it down the middle. One part is the so-called Eastern Shore, so-called because it's far broader than a shore; the other part is the western shore, which is also far broader and so has been called in recent decades "Southern Maryland."

The reactions of the opposing shores to economic conditions have been illuminating. Starting in colonial days the farmers on both shores had grown tobacco as if no other crop existed. The Eastern Shore even now has a reputation for rejecting change, and yet after the Civil War the farmers of the Eastern Shore gradually turned to the cultivation of very appetizing vegetables and fruits. While the profits from tobacco had shrunk with the passing of the decades, the profits from the vegetables and fruits were increasing. They could be sold either fresh or canned, and when the twentieth century started, Maryland led all the states in the canning of tomatoes and beans and came second only to California in the canning of fruits. On the other hand, the farmers of the western shore, though they weren't cut off from the rest of the state by the Bay as the Eastern Shoremen were, clung to tobacco. The men who bought the tobacco from them had many profitable years, right into the twentieth century, but the farmers themselves seldom made more than a meager living. Today farming in Southern Maryland is being crowded by the service industries, since much of the area is a dormitory for Washington and dormitories need services. However, some of the farmers are finding consolation in the fact that, even if there's little money in farming, there's a good deal in selling farm land to the real estate developers.

The watermen, unlike the farmers, have had the same luck, good and bad, on both sides of the Bay. After the Civil War seafood harvesting continued to flourish; Chesapeake oysters were fea-

tured in the restaurants not only of Baltimore but of Philadelphia and New York. However, there were as many unpredictables involved in harvesting the water as in harvesting the land; and a lobster could be as vulnerable to disease as a tomato. Equally if not more important, the Chesapeake watermen exploited the water just as the tobacco farmers did the land. They worked it too hard, so it yielded less. The result today is that fishermen's luck isn't what it used to be.

Till quite recently the social changes on the Coastal Plain have differed from the economic ones. The Eastern Shore, on balance, was progressive economically but conservative socially. The western shore, Southern Maryland, was conservative in both respects. Now, led by Charles County because it's nearest Washington, it's being swiftly urbanized. As far as we can tell, the effects on the whole are good. However, more than one old-timer has been heard to grumble that the county is being inundated by commuters from the Federal City who speak a bureaucratic lingo and have a bureaucratic view of life. While the social changes on the western shore are sweeping, those on the Eastern Shore are relatively slight. There, the farther south we go, the more we find old-style opinions and attitudes. In fact, we can even find traces of old-style English in the Shoremen's speech. They're still apt to say "neither" for "no" as did their forefathers: "A man wants to follow the water, ain't neither way to keep him ashore."

Geographically Baltimore belongs to the zone of the Coastal Plain. In actual fact it influences, and in some ways even dominates, all the zones. True-blue Baltimoreans believe that it *is* Maryland. Its shipping, because Baltimore ranks as a national and international port, helps to determine the shape of the state's economy. Its industry is the leader of the state's business. Its sheer bulk, as Maryland's only metropolis, affects the political and social structure of the state. Even its cultural institutions reach beyond the bounds of Baltimore. Each season the Baltimore Symphony, for example, gives concerts in counties as far off as Somerset or Cecil. Baltimore's way of life is inescapably metropolitan.

The Piedmont Plateau boasts the richest fields in Maryland. Small wonder that, starting in colonial days, they lured farmers from Pennsylvania and further away. The thrifty, sober Pennsylvania Dutch arrived first and set their stamp on the Plateau. The limestone soil of the gentle valleys practically guaranteed them the tallest corn and most abundant wheat in Maryland. The Plateau was also long admired for the sleekness of its herds. The undulations of the Plateau, with the aid of the fall line, furnished water power for the grist mills and small factories which were built in the area. Today the grist mills are almost all closed, having long since been replaced, mainly by cotton mills; but some of the factories have survived, and more than a few have prospered.

Manufacturing has come to outstrip farming as the chief economic activity, with products ranging from airplanes to underwear. The Piedmont counties have worked hard to bring in more manufacturing to offset farming's decline. One county hasn't had to. Montgomery, the Piedmont's southern sector, has had enough high-priced suburbs as well as high-tech industries to make it one of the wealthiest counties in the United States.

In the Appalachian region mining, mostly of coal, has remained the major industry for 150 years. Throughout the decades it had its ups and downs; however, in the middle third of the twentieth century it experienced a depression from which it has never quite recovered. Although the gasoline shortages of the 1970s caused some mines to reopen, their profits proved to be less than anticipated. Because of the brief growing season, farming does well only in a few valleys, chief among them the Hagerstown Valley. Nearly all the area is mountainous or high-plateau and much of it is covered with trees. Historically lumbering has rated as the second industry after mining; but for the most part its profits are tied to the prosperity, or the lack of it, of the building trades. Though the social effects of a depressed economy are naturally grim, one has the feeling that the region is making out better than might be expected. The people are active and are helping each other to an exceptional extent. The farther west one goes, the more apparent the region's hill-country culture becomes. It's marked by a clannishness that puts off outsiders but makes for solidarity within the clan.

Despite its problems Appalachia shares in Maryland's vitality. And the beauty of much of the region is incontestable.

* * *

Essentially we'll be describing the Maryland of today. However, there's a certain amount of yesterday that deserves to be noticed. After all, we're into our 350th anniversary, and the past helps explain the present. At any rate we can go back far enough, to begin with, to see the state through the eyes of its liveliest, most rambunctious writer, H. L. Mencken, who lived in contentment on Baltimore's Hollins Street from his childhood in the 1880s till his death in 1956.

He saw the state shrewdly, I think, as a mixture of stability and change, historical continuity and recent innovation. He also saw it as a state of contrasts in general.

He could admit that parts of Baltimore not only looked shabby but appeared determined to stay that way. But the rest looked comfortable, even comely, Mount Vernon Place above all perhaps. He found the villages and farms encircling the city a feast for the eye. The main roads leading from the city were also attractive, with a single exception. The road to Annapolis lay through

wooded heights and pretty valleys; the road to Frederick, he exclaimed in the *Evening Sun* for September 15, 1916, was an "avenue to enchantment;" but the road to Washington was unbelievably ugly. It still is; the state doesn't have a more garish highway than Route 1. Autobody shops crowd between filling stations and squat motels, while the asphalt ribbon snakes along between hedge-rows of neon.

Mencken was a prejudiced man and proud of the fact, for he entitled his series of books of essays *Prejudices*. He was prejudiced against many things but not against Maryland. Yet he wasn't blind to its shortcomings; he had a sharp eye anyhow and he'd once been a police reporter. In his prime he entrained each fortnight to Manhattan to edit the *American Mercury,* which during the 1920s was the nation's most noted and notorious magazine. But he fled back to Baltimore the moment his job allowed. He said more than once that if he could slam his desk shut at 3 p.m., he would leap on the 3:25 train, eager to abandon a metropolis with no more charm than a circus lot or a flea-bag hotel. The New Jersey he would glimpse through his Pullman window on the ride home was a state gone to wrack and ruin; eastern Pennsylvania was devoid of warmth; Delaware was a mere blob. But ten feet past the Mason-Dixon line the fields grew greener and the little towns turned cozy.

Elsewhere the state was still better. To him the most beautiful parts of Maryland lay in the middle: Howard, Carroll, and Frederick Counties, the counties of the Piedmont. He liked Howard County especially, as he said in the *Evening Sun* for April 12, 1926, with its fat cattle grazing in the meadows, its sheep on the hills, and its noble groves of well-kept trees.

And Baltimore itself? Toward it Mencken felt love tempered by exasperation. In his younger days he complained about the stench of the Inner Harbor, the crassness of the city's political corruption, the smugness of its citizenry, the blight of some of its neighborhoods. In his later days he still complained about all these matters except the Inner Harbor, which no longer acted as the catch basin for the city's sewage. And he found new things to complain about, such as the disappearance of trolley cars and the advent of air pollution. Yet he wouldn't have lived anywhere else.

Even his complaints evidenced his affection, for he wished to make Baltimore better. The reforms he urged on the city over the years were rarely carried out, but they often had the merit of making sense. To take a salient example, he argued for forty years that Baltimore should build a subway, with four cross-town lines. And he was often shrewd about his predictions, for instance about the future gentrification of the inner city and the renaissance of some of the ethnic neighborhoods.

Understandably, as he grew older he grew less sanguine. In his salad days, though, nobody surpassed him in expounding on the amenities and prospects of Baltimore. When he worked for the *Smart Set* magazine, the predecessor of the *American Mercury,* he published a paean in 1913 that he called "Good Old Baltimore."

In this essay he announced grandly that Baltimore was the temporal capital of the New World and the spiritual capital of these United States. It was the spiritual capital because it domiciled the ranking Catholic prelate, James Cardinal Gibbons. It was the temporal capital because — well, because it had charm. Infinite charm. Among the things that contributed to the charm was the food. The restaurants and dining rooms served the most succulent fare to be found in the Western Hemisphere, and the best of it came from the blue waters and fertile fields of Maryland. Maryland terrapin, oyster pie, soft-shelled crabs, corn flitters (not fritters), pawnhoss, and a host of other specialties: the list was long and appetizing. Besides its famous food Baltimore provided an unostentatious friendliness and a mellow civilization.

What about Baltimore now, however? Today is a time when many of America's big cities are struggling to stave off ruin. The answer, which we can give with pleasure and relief, is that Baltimore is flourishing.

Suppose we take a look at the city in 1976, the Bicentennial year, to find out how this came to be. We might even do it from the perspective of Washington. No one has ever accused the nation's capital of viewing Baltimore with admiration. For all too many Washingtonians Baltimore is located just across the river from Kansas City. In the fall of the year the *Washington Post* dispatched an investigative reporter to Baltimore. Charles Krause came back with the news, published at considerable length on November 22, that the city was making it. "Baltimore Winning Fight to Stay Alive" the headline announced, but the story below went much further. "Baltimore's growing reputation as a vital, diverse, culturally rich and architecturally exciting city has made it the urban find of 1976." He sounded like Mencken.

Problems persisted of course, the problems besetting every metropolis. As the reporter noted, many of the poor were still confined to slum housing, including some of the alley hovels that had survived since Mencken's time. Moreover, year by year the poor had been increasing while the over-all population had been shrinking from 906,000 in 1970 to 844,000 in 1975. Most of the loss had been middle-class and white. The flight to the suburbs had been the standard one for the standard reasons: the search for better schools, the fear of crime. By 1976 the crime rate was falling but the educational rating of the schools hadn't started to rise. Notwithstanding, when profits and losses were balanced Baltimore stood miles above her sister cities.

Although plans to renovate Baltimore had begun a generation

earlier, much of the credit according to Krause went to recent leadership. Mayor William Schaefer had shown himself to be energetic and enterprising; in addition, he'd proved willing to give his public planners a free hand. The city had also benefited from the support of such far-sighted and civic-minded business-men as Walter Sondheim, chairman of the Charles Center-Inner Harbor Management, and his key aide Martin Millspaugh. The Center was close to completion, a handsome complex of 15 new buildings on 33 acres, strategically located midway between the financial district and the retail-stores district. Aimed at helping the city's ailing downtown, it already boasted a theater and hotel as well as offices and shops. One Charles Center was the most prestigious building. Designed by the noted Dutch architect Mies van der Rohe, it proved to be a prize-winner. Only a convention hall, among major structures, remained to be built.

Even if it no longer received the city's sewage, the Inner Harbor had been growing slummier each year. Krause reported, however, that the old port area, marked until recently by rotting piers and grimy warehouses, had now been transformed into a spectacular urban waterfront. A salient reason was the choice of architects. Just as Charles Center had been able to enlist Mies van der Rohe, the Inner Harbor drew on the talents of I. M. Pei and Edward Durrell Stone. The Baltimoreans managing these important mat-ters were not only doing good deeds, they were doing them with style. After all, van der Rohe, Pei, and Stone were among the leading architects in the world. By 1976 the Harbor area included Pei's dramatic World Trade Center and Stone's Maryland Academy of Sciences building, along with the towering Fidelity & Guaran-tee headquarters, a new Chesapeake & Potomac building, and parks, boulevards, and playing fields. An eye-catching aquarium was still to come.

But all this construction would be largely cosmetic unless more of Baltimore's citizens had a decent place to live. Many a poor family was existing in squalor. Mayor Schaefer appointed as Hous-ing Commissioner a local man with a Harvard law degree and extraordinary civic sensibilities, Robert Embry. He gave Embry orders to do all he could to better the way Baltimore was housed and assured him of unflagging support. Embry proceeded to develop a whole combination of creative ideas and then to carry them out in a way that brought him national recognition. For example, instead of building bleak and boxlike highrises for city-sponsored housing, he got the celebrated Moshe Safdie to design a novel development to be christened Coldspring. It would be a "Town in Town." It would have some highrises, true, but humane ones complemented by groups of houses on the slopes and "deck-houses," which were actually rows of town houses facing each other across a pedestrian deck.

Baltimore was widely known as a city of neighborhoods, each with its own flavor, and Embry kept this in mind while planning his housing tactics. Little Italy was somewhat different from the mainly Polish Patterson Park and so needed at least slightly differ-ent treatment; so did bluecollar neighborhoods like Hampden when compared with middle-class neighborhoods like Home-wood; so did old historical neighborhoods like Mount Vernon Place or Bolton Hill. A certain amount of fine tuning was in order.

The greatest creativity came in the treatment of the city's row houses, Baltimore's trademark. Instead of tearing down the shab-biest ones and replacing them with brick monoliths, the city pioneered in urban homesteading. It let prospective householders buy rundown row houses cheap in order to fix them up and live in them. A few sold for as little as a dollar. It did the same thing with detached houses. In addition, the city tried to lure some of the new suburbanites back into Baltimore by offering them imagina-tively designed new houses at bargain prices. The reporter from the *Washington Post* closed his article with a quote from Embry, "We have a long way to go but I think the trend is finally in the right direction."

There's been progress on multiple fronts. Baltimore hasn't turned into Utopia—for one thing, the downtown retail district is still in real trouble—but the housing and the Center and the Inner Harbor have succeeded just about as was hoped. The con-vention center is up and the futuristic looking aquarium has made a colorful addition to the Inner Harbor. It lures more than a million visitors each year. But the most important example of continuing advance is the addition to the Inner Harbor of Harborplace.

Splendid and monumental though the Inner Harbor is, it needed something to humanize it. The gifted Baltimore developer James Rouse devised it by creating Harborplace, which opened in July 1980. It's a pair of long, two-storey glass pavilions that are practically on the water. They contain nearly 150 shops and eating places. On its two levels the Pratt Street Pavilion houses all sorts of small specialty shops, selling everything from butterflies to leather apparel, along with several restaurants. The Light Street Pavilion is equally enticing. It has the air and bustle of a bazaar.

What makes Harborplace work is the visitors, who find it diffi-cult indeed to keep from turning into customers. Both pavilions have a cheerful, almost sensual appeal that offsets the impersonal dignity of the big new buildings. The effect is what I believe Rouse was after: an environment that makes people within it feel better.

Office buildings and housing catch the eye. Cultural achieve-ments naturally are harder to see. But they exist, and they reveal a city which may recapture the mellow civilization that so pleased Mencken in his younger days.

The principal cultural institutions are those of any metropolis, except that they seem better off. They include the Baltimore Symphony, Center Stage, the Baltimore Opera, the Baltimore Ballet, the Walters Gallery, and the Baltimore Museum. To expand their activities, not simply maintain them, they've been able to depend on several sources. Private philanthropies and city contributions have been the most noteworthy; but state and federal money channeled through the State Arts Council, and federal dollars provided through the Maryland Humanities Council, have helped substantially. Equally important, the public agencies have been able to donate dollars to grassroots organizations which rarely attract a philanthropist. To take one of the agencies during one year as an example, the Arts Council in 1982 assisted the Southeast Latino Organization, the Corner Theatre Projects, the Baltimore Film Forum, and many more. If we set them all together they indicate a definite improvement in the quality of life for a good many Baltimoreans.

* * *

Baltimore had the great good fortune to number among its citizens men of the caliber of Mayor Schaefer, Walter Sondheim, and Robert Embry. But its good fortune went even further, for it was the home and headquarters of James Rouse. His amiable, slightly rumpled appearance and folksy manner concealed one of the premier minds in his business. In ordinary circumstances he would have made a signal contribution to the Inner Harbor from the outset. But the circumstances weren't ordinary. He was immersed in fashioning a city on his own.

Rouse had grown up on the Eastern Shore and though he went on to make his career in Baltimore, he never forgot the placid, neighborly life of his boyhood. He made his early reputation as a builder by devising exceptionally attractive shopping malls and he went on to other and more varied commissions. Two things distinguished the environments he constructed. One was that they put people first, the other that they were commercial successes. In the early 1960s he showed his fellow townsmen what he could do when he created the village of Cross Keys, northwest of Baltimore and not far from the city limits. He took advantage of the hilly terrain to intersperse apartment buildings and town houses with stores and an office building complex. An index to his insight was that he made an inviting village square the core of Cross Keys.

It was while building Cross Keys that he conceived the idea of a whole city, a salubrious city, that would enhance the lives of its residents at the same time that it developed a large enough business and industrial base to make it self-supporting. The city would have another characteristic, especially important for its time: It would foster racial integration.

By then a wealthy as well as a visionary man, he gathered a planning group which, characteristically, he didn't have chaired by a bricks-and-mortar builder but by an eminent social psychologist. In meeting after meeting the group, made up of from fifteen to twenty specialists, hammered out the plans for the new town, which would be christened Columbia. The members included the editor of the New Republic; the former city manager of Oakland, California; and the commissioner for recreation in the state of Pennsylvania, not to mention a psychiatrist and a communications expert. But the guiding hand belonged to Rouse. For example, he believed that big was not intrinsically beautiful. He was ready, though, to accept a big structure made up of small units; so that was what the planning committee gave him. It recommended that the fundamental unit should be the neighborhood; above that, three neighborhoods could be collected into a village; and finally a dozen villages could be gathered into a city. The neighborhoods could be sizable just as long as the size was ameliorated. They could contain from 3,500 to 4,000 persons; the villages could contain from 10,000 to 15,000; and the city, before this century ended, could contain something over 100,000.

Each neighborhood would be residential, with a "convenience store" as the only business. It would have its own elementary school, plus playgrounds, parks, and a community center. Each village would have a small collection of shops; and the city itself would have the necessary business district and city center. The center would include an extensive shopping mall of the kind that Rouse knew how to build so well. And there would be industrial parks on the outskirts.

Though the compromises had to be considerable, the committee never lost sight of Rouse's ideal for a salubrious city. To supplement the grand design it worked out, it came up with small ingenuities. For example, to go back to the matter of size, the neighborhoods might prove to be so large that the inhabitants wouldn't be very neighborly. One device adopted among many was to cluster the mailboxes on the residential streets instead of putting each one squarely in front of its residence. Clustered mailboxes would mean that people had a chance to meet and chat while getting their mail.

Basic to the planning was the problem of the ideal site. Like Mencken, Rouse found himself especially attracted to Howard County. Still rural but obviously open to growth because of its advantageous position between Baltimore and Washington, the county contained the site Rouse desired. All he had to do was to buy it. However, that was far from as simple as it seemed. He had not only to find financing for so prodigious a venture; he had to keep the buying secret or else land prices would soar through the ceiling. In this critical matter he displayed all the cunning of a spy in the movies, with the result that when in due time he confronted

the Howard County Commissioners, he could tell them that he now owned a tenth of their county. On hearing that some 22 square miles belonged to him, the Commissioners reacted in a manner as if stricken by apoplexy.

The obstacles to reconciling the Commissioners to the new reality were formidable; the same thing was true for the county in general. Consequently, Rouse spent months journeying around the county in his tweed jacket and brown loafers while he preached his message to anyone who would listen. He encountered more than enough outraged objections but slowly his message sank in. He made two telling points, one of which depended on the other. The first was that growth was inevitable. No matter how hard the county tried, it couldn't build a fence high enough to keep away outsiders. Given that growth was inevitable, the county had two choices. It could opt either for the schematic growth of Columbia or the suburban sprawl that was marring Prince Georges County next door. In 1965 Rouse won and the County Commissioners passed the rezoning ordinance.

Today the city lives and breathes, an exceptionally satisfactory habitat. A helicopter view shows the downtown center, with part of it fronting on one of Columbia's three lakes. At the outskirts lie the industrial parks such as Oakland Ridge. Just outside of Columbia and situated to take full advantage of the city, lies General Electric's own park, costing $250,000,000 and representing the biggest industrial investment in Maryland's history.

Within the city there's plenty of space left and always will be if things go according to plan. The neighborhoods are developing nicely. Early on, Rouse decided to put the construction of housing into the hands of private contractors unconnected with his own company. The result was a variety of plans and models, ranging from single-family homes to highrise apartments. The architecture ranged from the quite ordinary, such as the Ryland Group's more or less Dutch colonials, to the Chadwick Court Villas with their tall, thin windows and contemporary lines. Some of the choicest housing went up, understandably, near the lakes.

And what about the people who've chosen to live in Columbia? Suppose we look at them in the first year of the 1980s and check the statistics. In that year 54,800 persons occupied 18,145 dwelling units. The typical Columbia family was relatively young, small, well educated, and well paid. The typical household had two adults and one child. The mean age of the population was a little over 37 years. Two-thirds of the adults were college graduates; about one-third had done postgraduate study. The mean income was $37,800. Unemployment was less than 1 percent.

Rouse was entitled to look on Columbia, it seems to me, with satisfaction; he'd gone as far as anyone could to make it work. Not that there wasn't still a distance to go. The city had suffered, at least to a degree, from the impact of two national depressions, the one in the mid-1970s and the other in the early 1980s. Then too, with growth had come crime, drugs, and vandalism. They'd been greeted by some of the townspeople with innocent surprise, for they'd assumed that things like that wouldn't be found in Columbia. Similarly, some of them had expected too much of their private life in the New Town. They discovered that living in Columbia couldn't cure a sickly marriage or straighten out a drug-addicted teenager. Furthermore, living in Columbia couldn't automatically resolve the race problem. The relationship between middle-class blacks and whites appeared to be as good as anyone could expect. But the white teenagers often felt that the black ones were truculent while the blacks felt that the whites were stand-offish. Everything considered, however, the reaction to Columbia throughout the city was emphatically positive. The most vital evidence: 80 percent of the residents reported that they'd commend Columbia to their friends as a good place to live.

* * *

Much of Maryland, led by Baltimore and Columbia, is looking to the future. Not Annapolis, and with good reason. Its city limits enclose more history than any other spot in the state. It represents a gratifying adaptation of the past — and this means the elegant eighteenth century even more than the florid nineteenth — to the uses of the present.

At the same time, it's no museum, no Williamsburg. Its narrow streets with their handsome houses are usually crowded, partly by tourists but mainly by members of three subcultures which meet here but seldom mingle. The subcultures are those of the Naval Academy, the politicians, and the indigenous Annapolis families.

When the leaders of the three groups meet, it's almost always with an air of amiability. However, rank-and-file minorities in each group view the other groups with mixed emotions and that makes life in Annapolis more interesting. Rumor has it that some members of the old families believe that all politicians wear polyester suits and are nicknamed "Al." Some of the politicians supposedly see the Annapolis families as uniformly sunburned and besotted by sailing. Some members of the Naval community wonder aloud why politicians don't shape up and show a little discipline. And to some of the captains and admirals the old families look like dilettantes. Notwithstanding, the city runs with surprising smoothness.

The politicians, headed by the governor, rule over the executive branch of the state government, and set policy for the state civil service. Equally if not more important, they make up the legislative branch in the form of the General Assembly. Inevitably, the Naval community is in the city but not of it, for it's made up of

transients. Some of the senior officers return to Annapolis, however, since they went through the Academy there. Meanwhile, it's the old families, on the whole, who keep the city going and they do it with the effectiveness of long practice. After all, such families as the Quynns provided leaders as far back as colonial days.

The fact is that Annapolis has been the capital during nearly all of its history. Its pattern of growth — its urban planning if you will — was set before the end of the seventeenth century. Just how it grew is lucidly explained by Edward Papenfuse and his associates in their *Maryland: A New Guide to the Old Line State*. A royal governor of the 1690s, Sir Francis Nicholson, decreed that two circles, now State Circle and Church Circle, should be laid out on the knoll at the center of town and that streets should radiate from each one. The pattern has endured till this day and gives the city much of its charm, if many of its traffic problems.

By the middle of the eighteenth century Annapolis was acclaimed for the elegance and fullness of its social life. In its way it tried to outdo London. Any visitor who kept a diary was apt to exclaim in it at the dazzle. Late in the century, on December 23, 1783, George Washington stood before the Continental Congress, meeting in Annapolis, to resign his commission as commander-in-chief. He was a visitor more than once and relished Annapolis society.

From time to time, then and later, Baltimore tried to pry away the state government from Annapolis but the city always fended off those efforts. Gradually the city declined as a port, as did the fortunes of the old families that had been based on selling seafood or growing tobacco. Enough money, however, and enough guile remained so that Annapolis stayed afloat. The development of the Naval Academy, starting in the 1840s, though sporadic, aided the economy and reinforced the city's prestige.

Today the city occupies a unique place in Maryland. Its ambience continues to be attractive and the tourists arrive in throngs. Besides tourism, the principal industries derive from the members of the three subcultures. The politicians provide a substantial payroll to be spent in Annapolis. They themselves require food and shelter as long as the Assembly stays in session; and they also have minor needs. Similarly, the Naval Academy and its community help to keep the city's economy going. And the old families manage the services that Annapolis provides. Not the least advantage of the service economy, as opposed to an industrial one, is the benefit of cleaner air. The city has its share of automobile exhaust but the air still smells good.

The prime distinction of the city is the remarkable extent to which it has kept and cherished its eighteenth-century buildings. They include both public and private structures, along with places of business. Many are handsome and several are breathtaking.

The State House is more than 200 years old. With the passage of time it has added an unusual number of decorations, starting with the elaborate wooden tower in 1783; but the result has been more pleasing than might be expected. The Governor's Mansion is another official building, dignified enough to suit almost any incumbent. It was opened in 1870, but in 1936 friends of the eighteenth century swept away what they considered to be Victorian clutter, replacing it with Palladian windows and other eighteenth-century features.

There's a nice balance of surviving inns and churches. The Maryland Inn is the most celebrated of the hostelries. Built in the 1770s, today it's a favorite of lobbyists for its fine food and congenial atmosphere. The Reynolds Tavern went up even earlier; it's a two-storey structure with, as the *Maryland Guide* puts it, "a dormered gambrel roof and broad end chimneys." The churches tend to be more nineteenth than eighteenth century. The original St. Anne's was completed in 1706 but the present building dates from 1859. With its clock tower and octagonal steeple it looks older than it is. St. Mary's Church, a Victorian-Gothic combination that works out unexpectedly well, was dedicated in 1860.

A small assortment of business buildings remains, among them the Middleton-Randall building. Two boardinghouses, once much patronized by politicians and visitors, the Frances Bryce and the Ghiselin, are worth noting. Thomas Jefferson boarded at the Widow Ghiselin's in January and February of 1784; he recorded in his diary that he frequently dined with the widow herself.

However, the architectural reputation of the city doesn't rest so much on public or semi-public buildings as it does on a score of distinguished residences, most dating from the eighteenth century, that have been preserved with loving care. They're nearly all built of Maryland brick, and the most distinctive style of domestic architecture in the city is what's called the five-part form. Its basics are a central block with a subsidiary building on each side, connected by a one-storey passageway. The most renowned of Annapolis houses, the Hammond-Harwood and the Paca, both employ this style.

The houses are the city's pride but the waterfront holds the city's recreation. The harbor, with its docks, often looks as crowded as the Annapolis streets. At the height of the sailing season hundreds of boats collect there. The Hinckley Bermudas, with all their teak, and the Whitby 42s are apt to be the most visible; but they're far outnumbered by the less expensive and consequently more popular boats, such as the O'Days in their various sizes and the Gulf Star sloops and ketches. On a sunny afternoon, they give the impression of a whole city afloat on luminous air and opal water.

Many of the tides of today have surged around Annapolis, leaving it relatively untouched. Road building and road widening have been limited. The four-lane highways connecting Annapolis with the modern world somehow seem to shrink after they enter the city. The Chesapeake Bay Bridge has had less effect than expected, for most traffic sweeps past the city on its way to or from the Eastern Shore. The bridge has meant vastly easier access to the Shore but not to Annapolis. That's the way Annapolis likes it.

* * *

Without doubt Baltimore, Columbia, and Annapolis all in their various ways qualify as success stories; they've done well. A look at other parts of the state reminds us that some always do better than others.

We recognize that some of our scenery is beautiful; some is commonplace. For example, the view from the "Narrows" in Allegany County is much more stirring than the view from the center of Smith Island in Somerset County. Similarly, some counties are flourishing; others are not. Montgomery County is floating in a sea of prosperity, while Prince Georges is hard put to meet its expenses. Charles County is booming and crammed with recent residents, while Kent is steadily losing population. Seen altogether they illustrate Maryland, providing the lights and shadows that give character to a portrait. Any picture of the state as it is today must include both.

Take southern Maryland. On both sides of the Chesapeake it's been undergoing a transformation, with mixed results. To comprehend it we need to work our way through a small thicket of figures and dates.

For well over two centuries Maryland was mainly agricultural and more people lived in the country than in the towns. Gradually, as America became industrialized, the population shifted. Yet it wasn't till 1910 that fewer Marylanders lived on the farm. Thereafter the trend away from the farm accelerated for half a century. However, the census estimates for 1975 had a surprise in them. Though the state's population as a whole had risen by 4.4 percent since 1970, Baltimore had lost a substantial 6 percent of its people. The same thing had happened in Prince Georges, one of the two dormitory counties that had long served the District of Columbia. In the other dormitory county, Montgomery, growth had shrunk to a trickle.

In rural southern Maryland, on the contrary, a change unprecedented in the twentieth century was taking place. Although five of the Eastern Shore counties had been losing population as late as the 1960s, by the 1970s they were actually gaining. Caroline County showed the most striking shift, from a 4 percent loss in the 1960s to an 8.6 percent gain in the first half of the 1970s. Even Somerset, least prosperous of Maryland counties, attracted 2.8 percent more people.

However, Somerset is Maryland's minority report and we ought to look at it for perspective. Somerset, making its living in much the same way since the seventeenth century, represents a stubborn attempt to stand still in an era of change. Its kindly climate and sandy soil have usually meant adequate crops for the vegetable farmers. But the harvests in the Chesapeake haven't been as reliable in recent years; neither oystering nor crabbing has brought the return the watermen hope for. Yet the watermen as well as the farmers try to keep their sons and daughters at home. It's probably true that most of the inhabitants, old or young, regard outsiders with wariness. The county retains its own well-marked subculture with an emphasis on local folklore and uncompromising customs such as saying grace before meals on many of the fishing boats. Somerset's official motto is "Semper Eadem," Latin for "Always the Same;" nobody doubts that the county means it.

Still, the outside world maintains an active outpost in Somerset; for the University of Maryland, Eastern Shore, has its campus in the town of Princess Anne. Its students for the most part are black but its leaders hope for a rise in white enrollment. As in Baltimore, two government agencies are trying to enhance cultural life in Somerset. The Maryland Humanities Council has been awarding the county seed money and offering suggestions for projects in the humanities. The State Arts Council has been awarding much of its grant money to the University of Maryland in Princess Anne; the rest has been divided between projects involving the whole Eastern Shore and those restricted to Somerset. In 1982 Arts Council money was allocated to the university for eleven performances by its drama society as well as for five art exhibitions, and two workshops organized by the art department; to the Fairmount Academy for an "1880s Festival;" to the Eastern Shore Symphony, and even to several events connected with the annual "National Hard Crab Derby."

Then there's Smith Island, nominally a part of Somerset County. It's to Somerset what that county is to the rest of the Eastern Shore. Lying in the middle of the Chesapeake Bay, it depends on selling its crabs and oysters—plus a touch of the tourist trade—to keep its fewer than a thousand inhabitants alive. It has three villages and, by one count, about five miles of roads. The roads don't even have names. The island has no government and the unifying institution is the Methodist Church; everybody belongs. The inhabitants are inbred and like it that way.

Ironically, less than 70 miles from Smith Island, on the Atlantic side of the Eastern Shore, lies gaudy, booming Ocean City. In recent years it has vastly lengthened along its glorified sand-spit, and its little streets bisecting the sand have been laid out farther and farther to the north. By now the street signs go right up to 145th Street and the Delaware border. Today the city perceives itself not only as a jam-packed summer resort but as a community where more and more people live year-round. The old Ocean City, with its carpenter-Gothic hotels for hot weather visitors, survives well enough. But north of it, large parts of a new city are being born. Speculators and developers have had a field day constructing costly condominiums. These huge boxes, some pyramid-shaped or L- or T-shaped, look like revivals of ancient Babylon or replicas of Mayan temples. But with wall-to-wall carpeting and heated swimming pools.

Yet signs of a more comprehensive city are appearing, a city mainly for retirees, though the summer is still dominated by the suntanned young. A year-round economy and something of a cultural climate are also being nurtured. In 1982 the State Arts Council helped finance chamber music and bluegrass concerts. There were also several art exhibitions, and some neighborhood projects have been locally organized. It's a beginning.

On the Chesapeake side of the Shore four counties fringe the upper bay: Cecil, Kent, Queen Anne's, and Talbot. Their scenery is some of the most pleasing in Maryland. It attracts through understatement. The essential quality of the woods, marshes, and streams is peacefulness; no Ocean City here.

In the society of the four counties we can see a peacefulness as well. The most telling statistics are those about population trends. Cecil has the largest number of people, plus the promise of the largest increase. In 1980 it had a population of 60,000 and 66,000 is projected for the next decennial census. Kent remains the smallest, with a population of 16,000 in 1980 and a projection of 300 less in 1990. In between those two counties, Queen Anne's had 25,000 people in 1980 and is supposed to go up to 31,000 in 1990. Talbot is supposed to grow only from 25,600 in 1980 to 25,800 in 1990. Static? Maybe. Or reassuringly stable.

The inland farmers and the Chesapeake watermen have had their ups and downs, so there's been a pool of labor, of varying size, available to both new and old industries. One of the chief industries has been poultry raising. It has prospered to such an extent that its production has outrun that of most of the eastern seaboard. Along with it food processing has grown, principally of poultry but also of seafood. Country Pride's broiler and processing plant is the main employer in Talbot County. Here and there in the four counties some heavy industry has been coaxed into operation. Among the more important employers have been Wiley Manufacturing in Cecil County, which does heavy steel fabrication, and Dixon Valve & Coupling in Kent County.

Tourism has done better. The boating, swimming, and recreational fishing — once the preserve of the year-round residents — have drawn more and more tourists. Although the season runs from Memorial Day to Labor Day the equable climate encourages both earlier and later visits. For tourists seeking natural beauty, the fall colors in the woods are especially alluring. For bird watchers, and goose and duck hunters, one of the most arresting events is the autumn arrival of Canada geese and other waterfowl by the tens of thousands. Their main flight path into Maryland lies along the Chesapeake, starting in Cecil County.

* * *

Unlike the upper Eastern Shore the lower one, except for the redoubtable Somerset County, has been the scene of lively changes. Yet lively though those changes are, they pale beside the ones occurring in Southern Maryland. Access has been of vital importance, and going to the Eastern Shore has meant crossing the Chesapeake Bay Bridge, a bridge that can all too easily turn into a five-mile bottleneck. Going to the western shore has simply meant sliding behind a steering wheel and doing some commuting. It may take a full hour from Washington to Waldorf, but that's been no deterrent to thousands of people. Of the three western shore counties Charles has been the most accessible; its northern boundary lies only a few miles downriver from the District of Columbia; practically speaking, all that commuters have to do is drive past the Beltway onto Route 5. St. Mary's County, at the southern tip of Maryland, is least accessible; Calvert County is in between.

The three counties making up Southern Maryland had two options as they moved into the 1970s. They could duck their collective head while a flood of newcomers washed over it or they could do what James Rouse had done. They could make plans. In a way, though, the problem was harder; for Southern Maryland was even less prepared for change than Howard County. Take Charles County for example. Its population had remained at roughly 24,000 from 1790 to 1950, then doubled in the next twenty years and tripled in the next ten after that.

Nevertheless, leadership emerged. This leadership was disparate and not always efficient, yet its achievements were and are impressive. We can find them reflected in the records of the historical and sociological project called "Southern Maryland Today," which was coordinated by Dr. Alain Dessaint at the Calvert Library in Prince Frederick during 1982-1983. Its background paper "Communities in Change" offers us an insight into the happenings in the area.

From the days of the first settlers, the economy had been basically agricultural, with tobacco as the key crop. Tobacco exhausts the soil quickly and for a long time the remedy was primitive: Move to fresh fields. Even when the farmers ran out of land they made adjustments with reluctance. Some turned to other crops, wheat in particular, but without enthusiasm. The other prop of the economy was fishing, fishing in the Chesapeake Bay and in the Patuxent River. Until recently, the water was less easily exhausted than the land, so fishing had fewer problems.

Today the tilt is away from tobacco and seafood and toward the service industries. The thousands of newcomers have brought with them multiple demands. We can see that all too clearly if we drive along Route 301 as it moves south from Waldorf to Newburg. Fast-food restaurants, dry cleaners, beauty parlors, taverns, filling stations, drug stores, supermarkets, motels ("by day or week"), discount houses, clothing stores, novelty shops: Route 301 has them all. Of course some were there before but never in such large numbers as exist today.

Just as the changes in the economy stayed slight for prior generations, so did the changes in the quality of life. No busy east-west or north-south trade routes existed, to be traversed by aliens with alien ideas. The three counties lived within themselves. The centers of life were the farms and the nearby small towns. The most memorable events were apt to be trips by steamboat to the big city, Baltimore. Although Baltimore was admitted to be an exciting place, coming back home was apt to be a relief.

The stability of individuals accompanied the stability of institutions. The things that people needed were both convenient and modest. The family, the church, and the school were all at hand. The family, with its full complement of three generations, usually occupied an unostentatious house. The local church was apt to be a simple structure. The schoolhouse had as a rule only one room and one teacher. There's a photograph taken early in the twentieth century, and reproduced in the leaflet *Southern Maryland Today,* that's an indication of those times. It shows tobacco still being hauled in from the fields by a double yoke of oxen. Still another photograph, from the 1890s, shows an old doctor, white-whiskered and benign, sitting in his buggy, doubtless on his way to visit a patient. It was a sizable step, a whole generation, from the 1890s buggy photograph to the Orange Crush truck photographed in Clements in 1926.

The truck was an omen, for the automobile went on to become the chief instrument of change. It began slowly but then came on with a rush. As late as 1940 the majority of families still didn't own an automobile. But after World War II automobiles multiplied, with an effect on almost every facet of Southern Maryland life. Institutions that had been rock-solid started to show signs of wear.

Only the government grew bigger and stronger. Mainly because of the war, federal authorities set up half a dozen armed-forces installations. In 1942 they established a naval base in St. Mary's County in what is now Lexington Park. It has developed into the dominant economic resource of the county, and it's been the automobile that has made it accessible to workers for many miles

around. Charles and Calvert Counties also became the site of installations, among them Indian Head, Webster Field, Solomons, and Randle Cliffs.

Because of the automobile, in large part, families became less cohesive; church attendance became less frequent; the little white schoolhouse gave way to consolidated schools. At strategic spots supermarkets opened. Entertainment became easier to get to; movies came closer, often within a half-hour drive. And, especially among young people, standards of conduct began to be unsettled. The automobile was an opportunity, and it didn't take long for active teenagers to realize it. In other words the twentieth century had reached Southern Maryland.

Washington's prime industry is government and government has been crucial to Southern Maryland since World War II. Through force of circumstance it has channeled thousands of its employees into the three counties to live. During the last few years the counties have been working hard to keep as many of the old ways as possible without losing the benefits of the new. The counties' leadership has come to see the issues clearly; and the issue encompassing all others is about the best way of life. The prime problem is the steadily swelling population. In this case, and in several others related to it, trade-offs are involved. An increased tax base has to be measured against subdivision clutter. Wider job markets have to be set against the loss of stability. Bigger federal payrolls have to be balanced against greater federal intervention in local matters.

However, thanks in good part to planning, the growing pains are being endured and in some respects are certainly lessening. The most visible and convincing evidence is the New Town of St. Charles. It's essentially a dormitory but its developers have made provision for the amenities of daily life.

St. Charles is situated on 9,000 acres lying about twenty miles south of Washington. As of 1982 its population was 17,000, of whom all but a few thousand of the workers were employed outside of the county. The main roads they traveled to Washington were Routes 301 and 5. Full then, they now are fuller.

Commuting problems aside, the organization of St. Charles is similar to Columbia's. Neighborhoods are designed to be about the same size as Columbia's, with each having its elementary school and convenience store at the neighborhood center. Three neighborhoods are to be gathered into a village, and each village will have, according to the prospectus of the builders, a center "containing educational, commercial, cultural, and health facilities." Most of the houses built so far are of traditional colonial design, and an effort has been made to save as many trees, mainly pine and oak, as possible.

Life on the water has also changed, though considerably less.

We recall that, as seafood has become scarcer, the watermen's life has grown harder. One other change is worth noting thanks to its implications for the future. Since the early 1980s women have been venturing into maritime occupations that had always been the domain of men. A few hardy women have been tonging or scuba diving for oysters, or crabbing from their own boats, or even skippering an occasional excursion boat or running a ferry. Most have been young and all of them have been lively. They *had* to be. Cheryl Phipps, for instance, has served as skipper of the Harbor Queen; Valerie Bittner, further up the Bay, has piloted the Oxford ferry. There's no doubt that they'll have successors and numbers of them. More cap'ns every year.

* * *

In Prince Georges and Montgomery we find another pair of illuminating contrasts. Though the two counties lie next to one another and both bound the District of Columbia, they are different indeed, geographically, economically, and culturally.

In 1900 Prince Georges was a combination of three elements: bluecollar communities close to the District's northeast line, estates and large tobacco farms in the southeast sector of the county, and small tobacco farms in the rest. Each element had its own viability. The workingmen populating towns like Mt. Rainier and Brentwood were in the main artisans whose ambition was to own the little houses they lived in; their neat lawns symbolized their self-respect. The tobacco farmers had to drudge long hours for their living and were at the mercy not only of the weather but of the vagaries of the tobacco market. The old elitist families of the southeast led a pleasant life, spent in their own limited circle. They controlled the county, and sometimes more; the Bowies, for instance, provided two nineteenth-century governors. They kept the county seat at Upper Marlboro, a small tobacco town, for their convenience instead of letting it go to the center of population, Hyattsville. However, the image of the county—in the eyes of the District—was always bluecollar rather than elitist.

In Montgomery the opposite has been and remains true; the image is one of affluence and liberalism, middle-class and upper-class. I say this with a touch of envy since Prince Georges is my county, and I don't disdain the advantages enjoyed by Montgomery. Still, in Maryland more than in some other states, the past has a way of dictating the present; so the roots of the difference between the two counties go deep, and the difference itself is very difficult to alter. At the start of the century the most obvious subculture in Prince Georges was white working-class Southern. In Montgomery it was white middle-class New England. Later on two important ethnological additions took place. In Montgomery it was a middle-class Jewish influx beginning in the second third of

the century; in Prince Georges it was a black working-class influx beginning in the final third of the century.

For Montgomery the original distinction between its subculture and Prince Georges' is clearly indicated in Ray Hiebert's and Richard MacMaster's thorough *A Grateful Remembrance: The Story of Montgomery County,* issued in 1976. Some of the signs noted in the book are trivial; others are not. But they're internally consistent. Around 1900, the Ladies Village Improvement Society of Linden was raising money to improve the neighborhood walks and roads. The women of St. Paul's Methodist Church were serving a New England dinner to pay for carpeting the parsonage. The Kensington Hall Association was erecting a town hall for lectures and civic meetings. Undergirding such projects were the voluntarism and town-meeting orientation of New England, which was carried from there to other parts of the country. This was the philosophy preserved in the spacious houses going up over the District's northwest line from Bethesda to Silver Spring. Beyond lay farm after farm in the rich, rolling Piedmont. But it was the early suburbanites, not the farmers, who increasingly set the tone.

Before World War I the development of the new suburbs was regulated solely by the developers' desire for a market; fortunately for the county, the best market was middle-class and above. The big houses provided an adequate tax base and the householders wanted a growing number of services for their money. They wanted schools, for one thing. Plainly, the rising population had to have more and better services. Schools, roads, sewers, fire and police protection all were needed and all involved a certain amount of planning.

The residents of these suburbs were especially good at planning, and they had no hesitation in trying to get the County Commissioners to implement their plans. In their providential New England way, the residents foresaw how growth was apt to take place in Montgomery even if they couldn't foresee the astonishing rate of increase. Also, they were lucky. Even early in the century the shrewdest developers, impelled by enlightened self-interest, made an attempt to provide some of the amenities of suburban life along with the necessities. They dedicated part of their land, when they subdivided it, for parks and schools; they constructed the interior roads and storm sewers; they even in some cases put the utility lines underground for appearance's sake. Their actions helped to set a pattern that even the crassest of developers had to take into account. It wasn't till the late 1940s that those developers who tried to squeeze in the most housing finally succeeded.

It was always true that such developers could call on political allies and that over the years they won some tardy victories. However, the ablest politicians tended to be on the suburbs' side and they had the help of the burgeoning civic associations.

Several of the old county families had long provided political leadership, none more so than the Lees. For the first decade and a half of the century, Blair Lee dominated the politics of much of the county. He'd been a classmate of Woodrow Wilson at Princeton and was a member of the Washington elite. Although he lacked the common touch, his other political skills made up for it. Through his influence in Annapolis he managed to see that a substantial amount of reform legislation was passed by the General Assembly. One of the most significant items was a measure allowing home rule for those counties that wished it. In later years Montgomery offered an example to other counties of how to create a soundly functioning self-government. In 1919 Blair Lee's son Brooke, a decorated hero of the war, returned to help his father. Brooke Lee soon displayed an ability to organize and to get things done that distinguished his career till his retirement.

The county's political machines varied in their nature and effectiveness but they all had to recognize the power of the civic associations. As early as 1925 enough of these had emerged to make an umbrella group advisable, so the County Civic Federation was formed. A number of the associations acquired a particular character because of the abundance in them of middle-class women with brains, ideals, and time to spare.

Women like Margaret Schweinhaut and Stella Werner, both homemakers to begin with, established a tradition of political action, with, as one of their most useful tools, the League of Women Voters. From the outset they went to work not only on the issues customarily considered their preserves, schools and libraries, but on economic and purely political issues. They ran up a record of solid reform.

The central issue for the county has been the nature of growth. Although the political and social wars about it have been various, there's no doubt that the way growth has been channeled has been the county's major asset. Land development has become the county's biggest industry, and it has generally reaped the rewards of thoughtful planning.

The rewards have been remarkable. The federal government, under orders after World War II to disperse its facilities, saw in Montgomery and especially along the corridor that's now Route 270, an attractive site for federal business and an attractive area for federal employees to live in. From the county's point of view the federal installations that arrived were equally attractive. They weren't the Government Printing Office or the Main Post Office with their host of bluecollar workers, but the Atomic Energy Commission or the Bureau of Standards with their bureaucrats and technocrats. The oldest and perhaps the most prestigious arrival was the National Institutes of Health, situated in Bethesda. It had moved there in 1938 and began an extensive expansion in 1959. Among the newer arrivals the Department of Energy, with its imposing facility in Germantown, was especially notable.

With federal installations came new businesses to serve the federal government. Vitro Laboratories, for instance, ranked as the county's largest private employer in 1960, and its Navy contracts included systems engineering for the Polaris submarine. The Airflow Company in Rockville in its very first year won contracts for ground support mechanisms for the Atlas and Titan missiles. These were young companies and nimble because of their youth. But in 1959 the county also attracted the long-established giant of American high technology, IBM. It opened the first of what proved to be a series of centers in the area. It wasn't long before the fancy buildings along Route 270 became a Who's Who of high technology.

The services offered to the county's new and old residents were appropriately high-level, right up to the latest and trendiest shopping mall. In the early 1980s that was White Flint, in the Rockville area; Bloomingdale's of New York put the ultimate stamp of approval on White Flint by locating a branch there.

Though the cost of housing continued to rise, houses continued to be built and bought. Viers Mill Village had no real successor in its mass production of houses. However, the county's longstanding opposition to apartments was nullified in part by general economic and social conditions over which it had no control. The result was that by 1970 a third of the total housing units in the county were apartment buildings. The pressures to provide decent housing for blacks and other minorities grew more powerful, though even today the minority population is small, with much of it concentrated in a few neighborhoods.

Meanwhile, Prince Georges was moving closer to the American mainstream. At the end of World War II it had at least some of the opportunities for intelligent development that presented themselves in Montgomery County. There was zoning; there was a master plan. However, the leadership in Prince Georges proved to be parochial and, even though the old county elite had to share some of its power, little improvement took place.

Under the guise of aiding the returned veteran to find a home for himself and his family, the county government approved zoning variances almost anywhere the developers saw a chance for profit. They proceeded to reshape much of the county. University Lane, for instance, swelled from a narrow road, running past meadows and marshes, into a broad highway that was renamed University Boulevard. On either side of it buildings went up, casually and fast. Filling stations and restaurants alternated with small subdivisions of small houses and acres of so-called garden apartments. These were three-storey red-brick buildings with minimal amenities. Developments like Viers Mill Village sprang up especially in the northern part of the county. Families poured in, and at one point in the early 1950s the county's School Board was opening up one new school every month.

The most significant social change occurred at the county's southwest corner. Blacks from the District began to move in and have continued, till today Prince Georges is nearly one-half black. Two of their reasons for leaving the District were the same as those of the whites in Baltimore: the fear of crime and the hope of finding suitable schools for their children. To these one more was added: inexpensive housing. Subsidies from the federal government provided apartment living for some of the most vulnerable members of the District's population—the elderly and the single-parent families with small children. Black power in Prince Georges is on the rise and considerable accommodation is taking place, with the black middle class acting more or less in liaison.

Unlike Montgomery, Prince Georges hasn't become the site of any of the federal government's high-tech agencies, with one splendid exception, the Goddard Space Flight Center. When the government hurriedly expanded its research on outer space in order to meet the challenge in 1957 of the Russian Sputnik, it fixed on 1,200 acres of federal land just beyond Greenbelt as the most suitable place for the Center. Named after Dr. Robert Goddard, known as "The Father of American Rocketry," it opened its first office buildings and laboratories in 1959.

Goddard's general mission is to carry out the most advanced studies possible in near-earth research and development. To be slightly more specific, it's responsible—as one of its publications tries to explain—for devising the technology needed to operate American spacecraft; for overseeing the industrial parts of the design and manufacture of the spacecraft; and for overseeing the worldwide tracking and communications network for manned and unmanned spacecraft. So far Goddard scientists and engineers have designed one-third of all the space experiments conducted on American satellites. These experiments have yielded a wealth of scientific information.

The National Agricultural Research Center at Beltsville is in its appeal the opposite of Goddard. With its well-tilled fields and herds of well-fed animals, it's always been a favorite place for parents to take their suburban-bred children on a weekend.

Do the farmers of America, and the rest of us who are their customers, want a more tender steak or richer milk? In the barns and pastures of Beltsville federal scientists, some of the best to be found anywhere, are laboring to produce them. Is there a call for plumper chickens with more white meat? They're being hatched in Beltsville. Do we want bigger ears of corn with juicier kernels or garden peas sweeter than before? The place where new crops are being invented and old ones improved is in the laboratories and fertile fields of Beltsville. Controversy sometimes plagues the Atomic Energy Commission, and we hear of moves to abolish other bureaus. But nobody, in politics or out, has anything but praise for what's being accomplished at the Agricultural Research Center.

One of Prince Georges' chief resources has been the main campus of the University of Maryland, located in College Park ten miles north of Washington. Its facilities have offered an intellectual, social, and economic stimulus to the county—and the state—from the late 1930s on. After World War II the university throve. Some critics had called it a "cow college" and during its earlier days in the century it had in some ways merited the term. After the war the curriculums diversified, the graduate programs expanded, and the standards rose. Student enrollment climbed from under 10,000 to between three and four times that many. The faculty and staff came to number several thousands. Students and teachers crowded the spacious campus and its broad green lawns and red-brick Georgian buildings. College Park gradually acquired ambitions to become more than a middle-level state university. Today its leaders are hoping to see it turn into one of the top ten state universities in the country. It's already superior in the sciences, especially physics and astronomy, and it's showing definite improvement in the humanities and some of the social sciences.

A cluster of middle-class residential communities has grown up around the campus; the residents are a conglomerate of faculty members, federal employees, and business and professional people. It's from these neighborhoods that some of the leadership for the occasional liberal movements in Prince Georges has been coming. A recent County Executive lives in University Park and has taught at the university. Faculty influence in political matters has been on the increase both in Upper Marlboro and in Annapolis though it can hardly be said to be great. On the other hand, the county and the state both need professional expertise, and that the university is furnishing more and more.

Though Prince Georges hasn't prospered lately, its prospects look good. I think that the excesses of past development are in little danger of being repeated. Taxes still present a problem but one capable of being coped with, given a measure of sacrifice. The political power of the county, based on a new sophistication, is making itself felt not only in Annapolis but at times in national affairs. By a minor irony the motto of Prince Georges is the same as Somerset's, "Semper Eadem," "Always the Same," but in Prince Georges it's becoming less so with the passing of each year.

* * *

If we had a prize for the county that established the most thoughtful balance between the old and the new, I'd recommend giving it to Carroll. Almost all Maryland counties are in transition,

including the counties of the Piedmont, which Carroll can represent; but Carroll's adjustment seems to me exemplary.

The symbol of Carroll's success is the Farm Museum, a mile south of Westminster. It's often a puzzling question about exactly when something should be put under glass, so to speak, for the edification of the future. For quite a while now, Baltimore's Children's Zoo has displayed barnyard animals since they've become as novel to city children as buffaloes or antelope. For Carroll the turning point arrived in 1965; that was the year the County Commissioners set up the museum. It was an acknowledgement that a habit of life, cherished from the time the first settlers came south from Pennsylvania, was on the way out. Not that it would vanish entirely, but any forecast of the future would envision the family farm's replacement by agri-business.

Since 1965 the Farm Museum has been receiving more and more visitors, and not only from Maryland. The farm itself dates from the mid-nineteenth century and its six-room house was finished in 1852. From then on it was a working farm till the County Commissioners transformed it into a working museum. The farm isn't absolutely typical—it's more sizable and more elaborate than most—but that's because it originally operated as an almshouse, where some of the county's poor could live and labor for their keep. Its model, however, was the ordinary, self-sufficient family farm, with all the ordinary outbuildings from barn to smoke house.

To enrich the museum by widening its scope, the county has added several craft shops, specializing in the farm crafts of the late nineteenth century. Consequently, the current complex includes a crafts building plus a broom shop and a blacksmith's.

With its undulating terrain the setting is lovely and pastoral. The farm and the shops are at their busiest in October, when the festival of the Fall Harvest Days takes place. All the normal farm and craft activities go on display. Though in actuality the farmers and their ever-busy wives were their own craftsmen, here specialists show the visitors how to do everything from quilting to blacksmithing to old-fashioned farm cooking. It should be recorded that the quilts are quaint and the apple butter tasty.

We find further evidence of the past and the effort to preserve some of its relics in the form of the grist mills and the railroad stations. They remind us that for generations the county depended heavily on its bountiful crops of wheat and corn, much of which went by train to such cities as Baltimore and Philadelphia. Union Mills, not far from Gettysburg, has a grist mill that for more than 100 years drew many a farmer with his wagon full of grain. Its history goes as far back as the last years of the eighteenth century, when the Shriver brothers, Andrew and David, erected the tall, brick building. Lee's Mill, south of Hampstead, is another mill still

left. According to the county leaflet *From Flume to Flour*, its wooden overshot wheel provided the power to grind wheat flour, corn meal, and hominy.

The Piedmont Plateau had just enough tilt so that the streams could turn the water wheels. The fall line helped too. Naturally some of the mills have long been gone, but about two dozen still exist and several have become tourist attractions. There's something about a water wheel and the old mill stream that appeals to everyone from landscape painters to picnickers.

Once ground, the wheat and corn had to go to market, and here is where the railroads came in. A network of little lines was laid, and during most of the nineteenth century they carried passengers as well as freight. Today what track hasn't been pulled up is overgrown with weeds. A few of the stations remain, however. Their architecture is what I'm tempted to call American Overdone. A bit fancy for their small size, they sometimes combine barge boards and brackets in an architectural anomaly. But the railroads were useful, and we can lament their loss in this era of automobiles and trucks.

The farmers who used the mills and railroads were mainly Pennsylvania Dutch, originally attracted by the rich soil of the Piedmont and the moderate climate. They brought with them, to Maryland's advantage, their characteristic traits of industry and thrift. English, Scotch, and Irish immigrants later joined them. They all lived a busy and relatively prosperous life, with the prosperity evidenced in Maryland as it had been in Pennsylvania by the big, imposing "bank" barns.

Gradually, throughout the decades, their pattern of life altered. As a rule, it wasn't a matter over which they had much control. The population trends of the twentieth century, we remember, favored the town at the expense of the country. Some of the young men who might otherwise have worked the family farm moved to the large towns with their industries, cash salaries, and excitement. So did some of the young women, though their opportunities were scarcer. In the last few years, however, Carroll's population has gone up.

Carroll County's leadership has been astute and read the trends clearly. Farming will never return to what it was, and the newcomers want jobs in modern industry. So the sensible thing to do has been to launch an aggressive campaign to draw as much new industry as possible, as other counties have done. In a recent brochure the county boasts its advantages: "Tax exempt financial assistance," it says, "may be obtained to acquire land, buildings, machinery, equipment, and supplemental working capital." It's hard to go much further than that, but as a matter of fact the county offers additional incentives.

They're led by the availability of industrial sites scattered

throughout the county, running from a single acre to several hundred, and by the presence of a substantial and growing labor force. For the prospective plant executives and workers the brochure describes—in what can only be called glowing terms—the housing, education, and recreation available to residents of the county. "Housing ranges from lavish estates and farms to modern garden apartments." Education is above the national standard and more than half the county's budget is allocated to it. And recreation? Everything from camping on hillsides of the Piedmont Plateau to enjoying "the cultural entertainment provided by touring and residential theatrical companies, ballet, symphonies, opera, or world renowned art galleries and museums."

On reflection we realize that all this comes as much from the nearby cities as from the county itself. Notwithstanding, the appeal has been persuasive. The clearest testimony is the plants erected by such nationally known concerns as Westinghouse Electric, Black & Decker, and Random House.

And one thing more. Like some of its sister counties, Carroll emphasizes the appeal of its way of life: "The blend of neighboring industrial hubs with the rural peace of the rolling hillside makes Carroll County the best of both worlds." Who's to say they're wrong?

* * *

Westward the state rises to meet the Appalachians. The Piedmont slowly slopes up; then come the foothills; and then the low, rounded mountains of the Allegheny chain. Allegany County is the middle one of the three counties of the western range, with Washington County on the eastern side and Garrett to the west. It can serve, even in some of its adversities, to represent the region.

Allegany is a county with enterprise and energy, fighting against bleak economic conditions. Unlike Southern Maryland its population is dwindling. It shrank from 84,000 in 1970 to 80,000 in 1980, and the estimate for 1990 is 77,000. The attraction of warm-weather areas has become nationwide and Allegany suffers from the fact. Historically its economy was based on iron and coal. Its famous Lonaconing Furnace was the first to produce iron by using coal and coke instead of charcoal. But that was before the Civil War and gradually only coal mining was left as the county's major industry, with lumbering coming second. Today mining is surviving but not flourishing, despite a temporary turn for the better during the petroleum shortage of the 1970s. And lumbering has been at the mercy of nationwide building trends. A cross-section of industries now located in the county includes the Kelly-Springfield Tire Company, the Celanese Corporation, and Westvaco, which produces pulp and paper. The county is engaged in trying to bring in more industry but with limited results.

Tourism, though restricted to summertime, has worked better. The scenery is often beautiful; the lakes are often bright blue, the streams sparkling. Much of the undeveloped county has been preserved in state parks and wildlife areas, among them the Green Ridge State Forest, the Warrior Mountain Wildlife Area, and Dan's Mountain State Park. Fishing, swimming, boating, hiking, and camping all bring in visitors. In the winter there's some good skiing.

There's also history for the history-minded. The county courthouse in Cumberland is a period piece in the Romanesque style of official architecture, with its big square tower and checkerboard bands. The tollgate house at LaVale is the only one left in the state from those built for the National Road. The Chesapeake & Ohio canal also has its relics. And for domestic architecture there's the Washington Street Historical District in Cumberland.

History of a basic economic and social kind is emblemized for us in "Prospect V-III," the most interesting and instructive piece of environmental sculpture in the state.

Set on a hillside on the Frostburg College campus, it's the work of the innovative Minnesota sculptor Andrew Leicester, and it opened in 1982. "Opened" is the proper word, for it's really a building or series of small buildings whose intention is to demonstrate, inside the structure and out, what coal mining is like. In a sense it sums up the industry. As one of the county publications says, it brings to mind the actual architecture of the mining communities that Allegany once knew so well.

There's the tipple, where the coal cars were loaded or emptied; the conveyors; the furnace, and a trio of company houses of the kind the miners and their families spent their lives in. Inside the structure a sequence of small rooms illustrates the various sides of the miner's life. The theme of the construction, according to the sculptor, is double: the human conditions common to mining and the transitions in humanity from birth to death.

Yet this monument to the past by no means tells the whole story of Allegany County today. Coal mining has always demanded grit, a tough, mundane courage; and that grit isn't gone. Though the challenges to making a satisfactory life in the Allegheny Mountains continue to be formidable, it can be sensed that a good many residents are meeting them.

The problem of earning a living is naturally foremost, but there's enough energy left over for the things that lead to a fuller life. To take one of my favorite indexes, cultural activities, the county isn't doing badly. Thanks to the County Arts Council and the State Arts Council, Allegany is enjoying its share of cultural events. In 1982 residents could attend a summer concert series by local performers in the Cumberland Mall; they could watch the productions of the Up Front Community Theater or of the Stage Left

Theatre; they could admire the craftsmanship of the Fibre Artisans; and they could enter a competition to identify historical landmarks, architectural and otherwise. However, the mountain culture still comes first.

In education Allegany Community College and Frostburg College are reaching out for students of diverse backgrounds and ages. Local chapters of the American Association of University Women and the League of Women Voters rank among the more active of community groups. A good sign that they're far from giving up was the program planned by the League entitled, "Parties, People, and Politics: Allegany County Faces the Future."

* * *

What's the most abiding impression that Maryland can leave either on its visitors or, when they think about it, on its residents? For me it's the continuity that goes with change. I find continuity nicely exemplified in the Arabers of Baltimore and the jousters of Oxon Hill. And change for me can be represented by all the improvements made in Baltimore in recent times and, more ambiguously, by the operation of the Calvert Cliffs nuclear plant.

Only a few miles from both the Inner Harbor and Charles Center, Arabers are still driving their horse-drawn wagons and following their long-time custom of crying their wares. We're not sure how they got their name; perhaps it derives from the vendors of the Middle East. An allied term is "street Arab," which was applied to vagabond boys, especially in New York in the late nineteenth century.

Folklorist George Carey, who has observed the Arabers for years, describes them in the *Johns Hopkins Magazine* of January 1976. They're street hawkers following an urban "tradition that is thousands of years old," according to Carey. Though they stand in the way of progress as defined by Charles Center or the Inner Harbor, they've managed to survive. They live by buying produce each day, vegetables and fruits, from the wholesalers and then selling it to customers in the inner city. They're up, driving their rickety wagons, by dawn, starting their search for the best bargains in the wholesale markets; but ordinarily they have to compromise by waiting to buy till mid-morning, after the fancy fruits and vegetables have been snapped up by the restaurants and hotels. Nevertheless, what they buy is edible and fresh as of the day.

In this era of bustle, technology, and nuclear power the jouster likewise survives. In most ways he's the opposite of the Araber, for he represents aristocracy, knighthood, and the pageantry of the distant past. But what the two have in common is a defiance of progress and what it stands for.

To do the jousting properly there must be a full tournament,

complete with a Queen of Beauty and Love to crown the best jouster and a Grand Marshal to preside over the actual jousting. The jousters usually give themselves high-sounding titles such as "The Knight of Valley View" or "The Knight of Little Woods" and they take the tournament seriously.

They have reason; for jousting, though no longer the blood sport it was in medieval days, still presents a challenge worthy of any knight from any locality. The target in Maryland has never been another knight but something far smaller and more difficult to spear. At Oxon Hill in Prince Georges County, in a typical tournament reported not long ago by Jane Seaberry in the *Washington Post,* three metal arches were set up 30 feet apart along a grassy track. At the end of the track several doughnut-shaped loops dangled seven feet above the ground. The largest loops were only two inches in diameter while the smallest were a quarter inch. Each knight was supposed to spear one loop at a time, starting with the largest loops on the first pass. He had to ride beneath the arches at full gallop, carrying his seven-foot lance under his right arm while guiding his steed with his left hand. His lance had a long metal spike at the end, with a point that was needle-sharp. To spear even the largest loops obviously called for superlative control.

The Oxon Hill tournament went off in style while 1,500 spectators enjoyed the revival of the past. But not simply a revival, for something new had been added in the last few years. It was the inclusion of women among the competitors, led by Mary Lou Bartram, who called herself "The Maid of Bartram Manor." Though she failed to finish first this time, the reporter found that she'd been a state champion three times in the past. But that's Maryland for you, slipping a bit of change into the continuity.

Right: Galloping out of the Middle Ages, the "Knight of St. Mark's," a self-bestowed title, becomes the state champion as he lances his last of the smallest loops, a one-quarter inch diameter ring. Although the front of the State Seal shows Lord Baltimore, founder of Maryland, as a knight in full armor, and the sport has been popular since he introduced it in the colony during the mid-seventeenth century, it was not until 1962 that jousting became the official state sport.

Below: What promises to be a perfect harvest moon rises above a weathered barn in Queen Anne's County, one of the least developed of the Eastern Shore counties. Out on Kent Island, twenty miles to the west, the moon once rose on the first European settlement in Maryland, a trading post founded in 1631 by William Claiborne. *Left:* When the fog burns off, this bare-branched tree and pond will test the skill of golfers at the Brantwood Country Club in Cecil County.

Below: An active participant in Ocean City's most popular sport. Over 150,000 people enjoy the ten mile long beach on summer weekdays, and weekends often attract 200,000. *Left:* The shallows and swamp grass in the backwaters around Assateague make a canoe the ideal boat for exploring or fishing.

Below: Maryland's log canoes have evolved from a mid-nineteenth-century Eastern Shore oyster boat to a racing craft unique to sailing. Every ounce of human flesh is needed to complement the wind, and every bit of concentration needed to stay dry. *Right:* Gulls feed and rest in a tidal inlet during an Assateague summer. *Overleaf:* A pumping barge plows through Chesapeake ice opposite Baltimore Harbor.

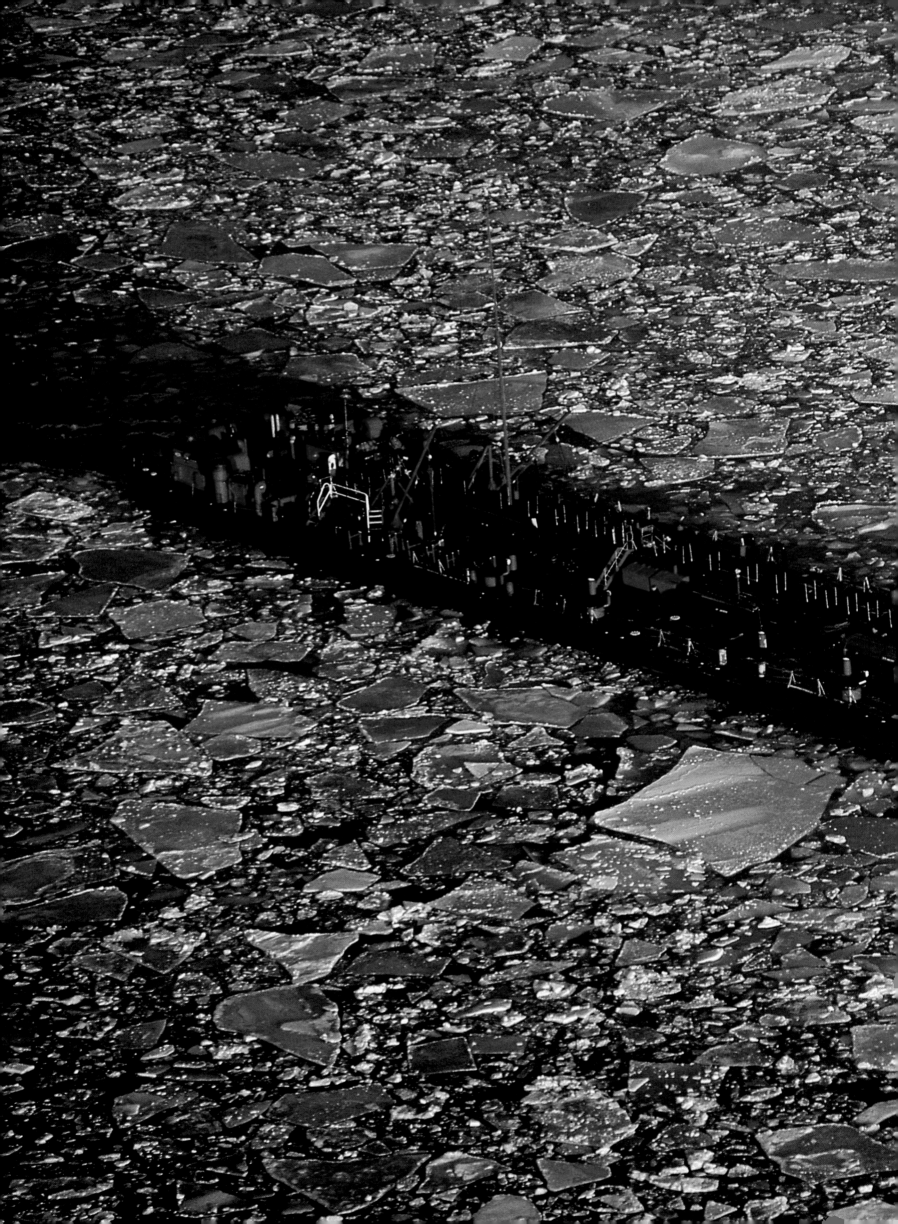

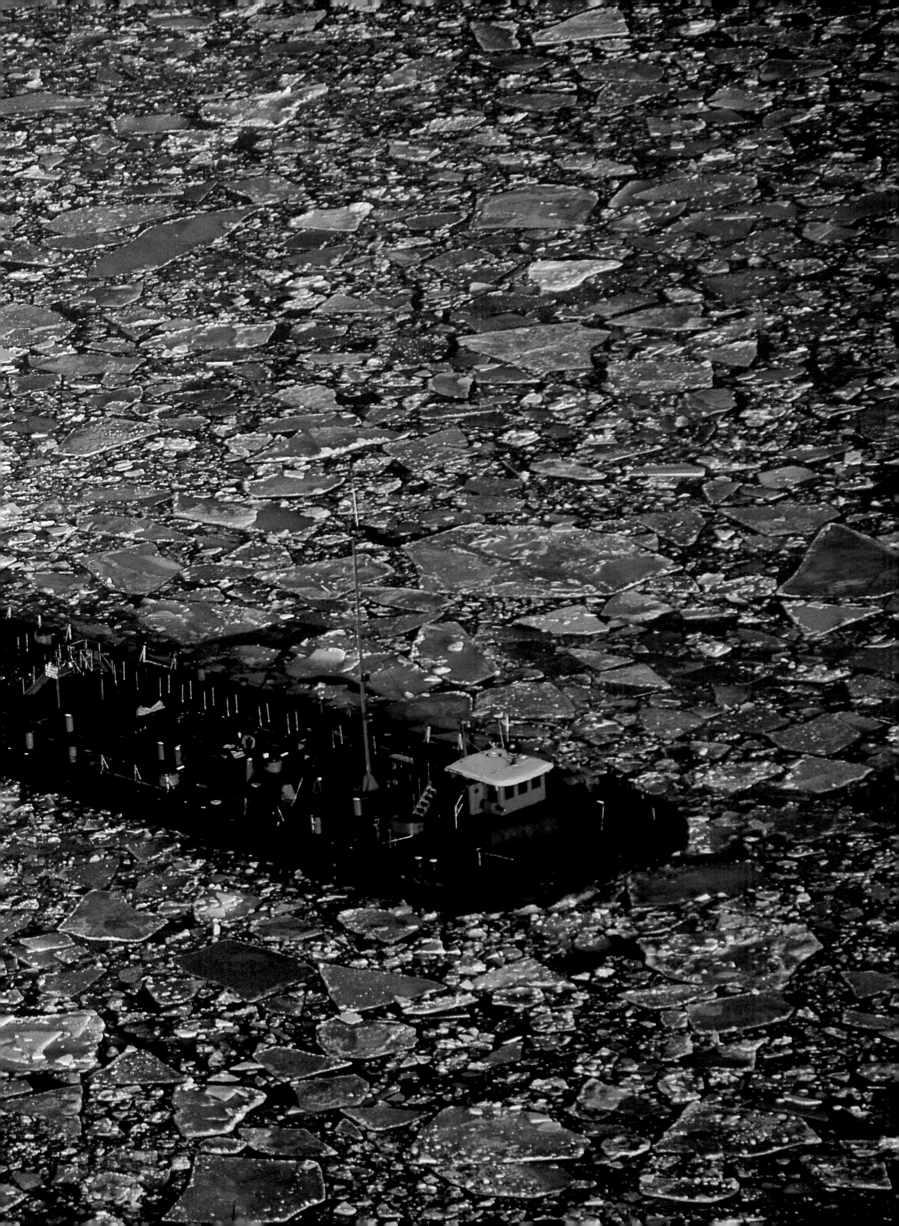

Below: The Eastern Shore continues to maintain its own tempo and sense of independence. Shore to shore service: An old-fashioned ferry, guided by a cable, traverses the Wicomico River at Whitehaven. *Left:* Tombstones surround the Asbury United Methodist Church in Maryland's own, modest Mount Vernon. *Overleaf:* Celebrating summer's end takes myriad forms on Labor Day weekend in Ocean City.

Below: One of Dorchester County's many examples of quintessential Eastern Shore. *Left:* The Wye Oak in Talbot County is more than four centuries old and spreads its massive crown 165 feet, making it one of the largest white oak trees known. The state bought the tree in 1939 and two years later made the Wye Oak and its kind, *Quercus alba,* Maryland's official tree.

Below: Sun and seagull: An unofficial symbol for a state that is one-fifth water makes an appearance over Sinepuxent Bay in Worcester County. *Right:* One of Chesapeake City's tin roof tops catches the Cecil County morning sun. Chesapeake City was the site of two of the four locks on the original Chesapeake and Delaware Canal when it opened in 1829. Today it is the site of Maryland's only remaining "piece" of the original canal, a gray stone pumphouse now converted to the Chesapeake and Delaware Canal Museum.

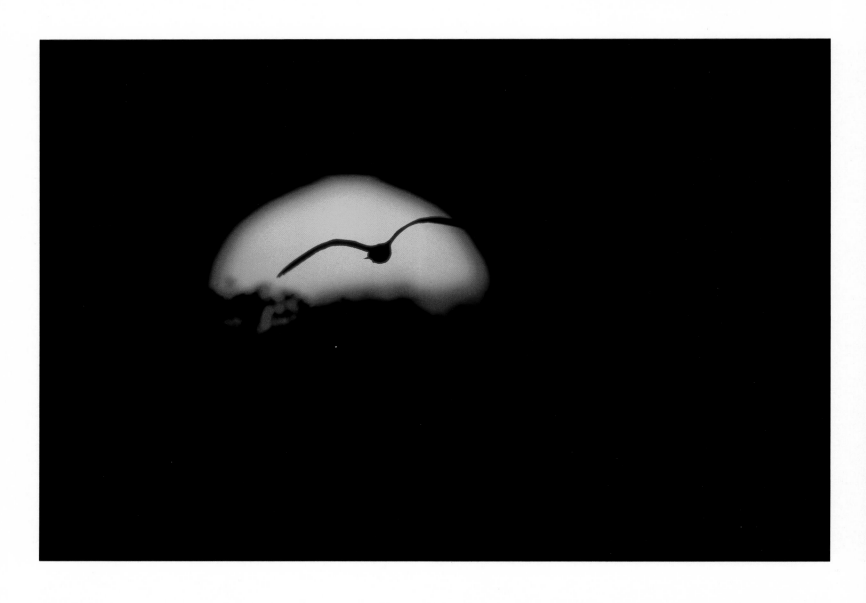

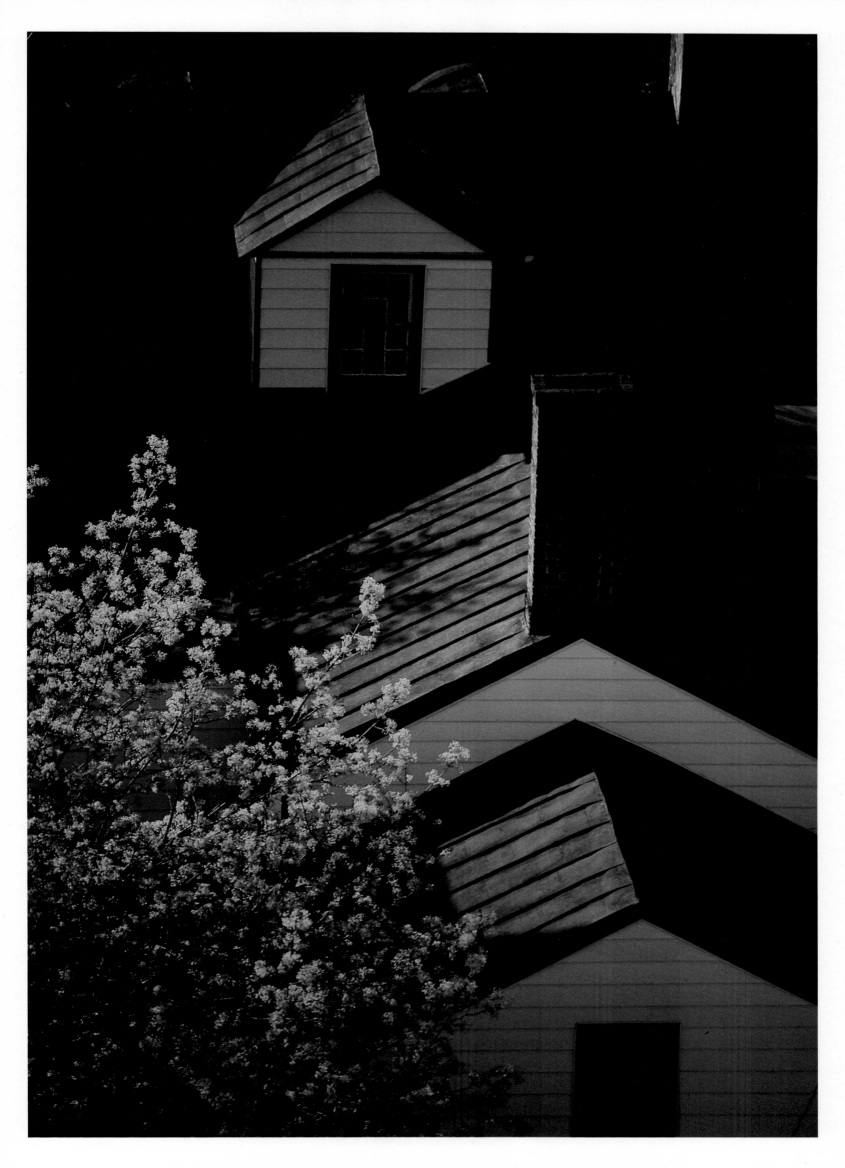

Below: These skipjacks competing in a traditional Labor Day race in Tangier Sound are part of the only sail-powered fishing fleet remaining in the United States. State law prohibits powerboats from dredging oysters in public beds. *Left:* A house in tiny Quantico in Wicomico County offers a study in blue on blue, cool on cool. The village is a delightful example of turn-of-the-century Americana, with its single street, country store, and cozy homes.

Below: Having raked up an adequate supply of Assateague shellfish, a family returns to camp for a clambake. *Left:* Every morning the national, state, and yacht club flags are raised at Schaefer's Canal House, a favorite stop on the Intracoastal Waterway. *Overleaf:* The wetlands of the Eastern Shore are the winter home for half a million waterfowl, one-fourth of which reside here at Blackwater National Wildlife Refuge.

Below: Pure exuberance, water-borne, male and female: a boat-to-boat greeting during a race on the lower Bay. *Left:* Log canoes, unique to Maryland, began racing in the 1850s, and some of the vessels in this race on the Miles River near St. Michaels are almost 100 years old. *Overleaf:* The Bay offers silhouettes of business and pleasure as the Skipper's Race passes through the tanker and freighter anchorage off Annapolis.

HEARTLAND

62

Below: In the tranquil light a descendent of a wild Assateague pony crops some herbage in Charles County. From livelihoods of farming and seafood, much of the heartland region has shifted toward an economy based on high technology and service industries. *Right:* A day of fishing comes to an end at Fort Smallwood at the mouth of the Patapsco River. One of the most important and valuable fish in these waters is the striped bass, or rockfish, *Roccus saxatilis,* which was designated Maryland's state fish in 1962.

Left: The rowhouse, fronted by its famous marble steps, is integral to Baltimore, combining neighborliness with privacy. Since many of Baltimore's ethnic residents share this same style architecture, neighborhoods become distinguishable only by the names of the family-owned businesses. *Right:* On hot summer days in downtown Baltimore, the activity moves outside where friends and neighbors sit and chat, enjoying each other and every cooling breeze that happens by.

Left: The toss of a hat marks the end of four intense years at the Naval Academy: Newly commissioned Navy and Marine officers fling high the final sign of their midshipman apprenticeship. *Right:* A park ranger plays the role of the post ordnance sergeant (1858 to 1862) at Fort Washington in an historical re-enactment that takes place on weekends from mid-April to December. George Washington selected the site for the Fort, which commands the Potomac for several miles in each direction.

Below: Though they may eventually command an enormous aircraft carrier, they begin with smaller craft: Midshipmen bury the lee rail of their Naval Academy yawl in one of the Fall Series races. *Left:* The three-day Great Ocean Race around the Delmarva Peninsula in May can attract half a hundred boats of different classes. Boats sail up the Bay after a start near Sandy Point Lighthouse north of the Bay Bridge.

Below: Lacrosse, the oldest sport in North America, was popularized as a collegiate game by the State of Maryland. In this contest, frequent national champion Johns Hopkins is beating Cornell. *Right:* The Pledge of Allegiance completes a tour at the birthplace of the Star Spangled Banner. In 1814 Marylander Francis Scott Key saw the American flag still flying above Fort McHenry after the British attack. His inspired poem became our national anthem in 1931. *Overleaf:* Independence Day at the Inner Harbor, Baltimore's renaissance at its best.

Right: The Color Girl assists the company commander (on her left) and the Naval Academy superintendent in honoring the outstanding company of midshipmen during the traditional Colors Parade. *Left:* Rapt in the music they're making, a pair of bassists play in the Baltimore Symphony, housed in the splendid new Joseph Meyerhoff Hall. *Overleaf:* One of Maryland's more recent rituals is the "Walk Across the Bay." The eastbound bridge becomes a 4.4 mile footbridge for 30,000 hikers who enjoy unique views of the Bay as well as the westbound bridge.

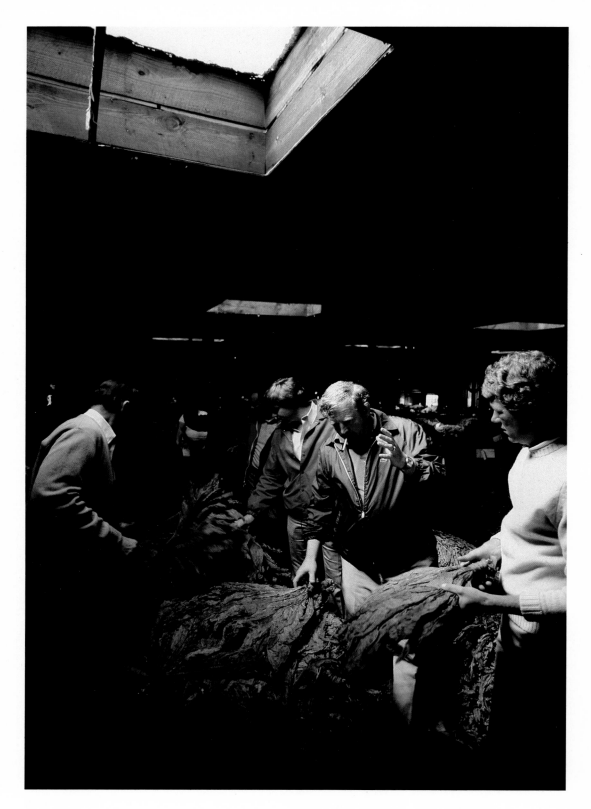

Left: Tobacco was Maryland's first, and once its foremost, cash crop. Today it's grown, though on a reduced scale, but still esteemed. In Upper Marlboro, the fast pace of an auction keeps bidders alert as they compete for the best leaf at the most favorable price. *Right:* At the University of Maryland in College Park, a student finds a tranquil moment in front of McKeldin Library to prepare for finals week. With an enrollment of 37,000 students, this bustling campus is the largest of Maryland's more than seventy colleges and universities.

Below: Wing on wing: An osprey family nests in the waters off Solomons, the southernmost point of Calvert County. One of several threatened species now seen in increasing numbers thanks to a ban on DDT, ospreys are a good omen about the health of the Bay. *Left:* The Maryland Hunt Cup Race, like most horse races, lasts only a few minutes, but most spectators make it a whole day of outdoor recreation — with picnics, frisbees, horseplay, and kites.

Below: A farmer fertilizes his field near Prettyboy Reservoir and Gunpowder State Park north of Baltimore. More than 16,000 farms dot the state and average about 170 acres in size. *Left:* Father and sons share the solitude of a winding rural road in Frederick County.

Below: A bee investigates a water lily on a fish pond at Lily Pons, a Frederick County community, named after the famous opera singer of the 1940s and 1950s. *Right:* A ketch cruises home at the mouth of the Magothy River near Gibson Island. Many experienced boatmen consider the Chesapeake Bay the best cruising waters on the East Coast. *Overleaf:* Rising moon over the Inner Harbor. In the continuing development of Baltimore's core area there are plans to turn the ship Nobska into a restaurant. The building beyond it houses the Public Works Museum.

Below: Featuring produce fresh from the fields, this roadside stand in Carroll County entices all who pass by. In addition to this produce, wheat and oats are grown in abundance, making farming second only to manufacturing in the heartland. *Left:* The Inner Harbor on July 4th, as jammed throughout the sunny day as in the fireworks-filled night. *Overleaf:* Under the glass pyramid roof, millions of visitors see Baltimore's own tropical rain forest and many other wonders of the water world displayed in the National Aquarium, the Inner Harbor's most striking structure.

Below: Montgomery County is home for the Who's Who of Maryland's high technology base. Achievement-oriented people garnering top salaries, bonuses, and perks make the county's average per family income one of the highest in the nation. *Left:* The envy of other cities: Propelled by its economic and social renaissance, the momentum of Baltimore's growth and improvement extends from the Inner Harbor to the outskirts of the city.

Below: With a variety that would almost satisfy Noah, animals on a farm in southern Prince Georges County gather for feeding time. Though the county has become suburbanized, farms like this still can be found almost within eye-range of the Capitol. *Left:* Riding the tractor he drove as a boy, this gentleman toots around the Steam Show at the Carroll County Farm Museum. Rubber tires replace the original steel wheels to prevent road damage.

Below: Control room monitors at the Goddard Space Flight Center in Prince Georges County show the final test flight of the Space Shuttle coming to a successful conclusion. *Left:* The Bethlehem Steel plant on Sparrows Point just south of Baltimore has the largest iron-producing blast furnace in the Western Hemisphere and at full capacity employs 25,000 workers.

Below: Edgar Allan Poe, Babe Ruth, and H.L. Mencken are a few of the famous Baltimoreans to have lived in a row house, the frontrunning style of city architecture for 200 years. History may someday record a famous occupant in one of these new houses on Monroe Street in West Baltimore. *Left:* Conversation on a summer evening in Patterson Park, Baltimore's noted Polish neighborhood. *Overleaf:* An alternate form of canoeing the Susquehanna: Between Port Deposit and Havre de Grace, two highway and two railroad bridges form a steel matrix across the river.

Below: Even though Baltimore Harbor has the facilities to simultaneously handle 200 vessels, 4,500 ships call annually. Those waiting their turn in port anchor off Annapolis. *Left:* Opposite the Great Falls of the Potomac, a boat is drawn toward Georgetown on the Chesapeake and Ohio Canal. Its name indicates the dream. The canal never reached the Ohio River, though by 1850 it was built as far as Cumberland. *Overleaf:* Almost eleven million vehicles annually cross the Bay Bridge. The population of the state is only slightly more than four million.

FOOTHILLS AND MOUNTAINS

Below: A capering canine appears unconcerned by the temperature which is well below zero. Nearby Oakland recorded the lowest temperature in the state to date: −40°F. on January 13, 1912. *Right:* A field near Hancock is nearly as long as Maryland is wide. The Mason-Dixon line and the Potomac River converge to within two miles of each other at this point creating a cartographic curiosity.

Below: Farm sheds near South Mountain. Nearby the Appalachian Trail meanders thirty-eight miles across Maryland, one of fourteen states along this 2,000 mile footpath. *Left:* A blood red sky at Antietam is a fitting background to remember its Civil War history: The battle between the North and the South on September 17, 1862 saw 26,000 Americans become casualties, 2,200 in just twenty minutes. It remains the bloodiest day of fighting on the North American continent.

Below: The black-eyed Susan, *Rudbeckia hirta,* blooms almost all summer and can be distinguished from other members of the sunflower family by its ten or more petal-like rays and chocolate-colored, cone-shaped center. Since 1918 it has been the official state flower. *Left:* Although corn is Maryland's leading cash crop, the old method of shucking is still evident in this Garrett County field. When the first settlers reached Maryland's shores in the 1600s, they found the Indians had cultivated corn long before their arrival.

Below: Although no battle was fought here, Ft. Frederick was completed in 1758 and served in colonial Maryland's defense during the French and Indian War. Summer reenactments bring alive both this period and the state's motto, *Fatti Maschii, Parole Femine:* manly deeds, womanly words. *Right:* Despite its name, Muddy Creek Falls in Garrett County, is one of the most picturesque in Maryland. Descending fifty-one feet, it is the state's highest waterfall. *Overleaf:* Cows graze a Garrett County ridgeline: more than 40 percent of Maryland is farmland.

Right: From the air these Allegany County fields fall into bold and simple patterns. *Left:* The best seat in the house during Maryland's extraordinary fall show of colors is in a private airplane. *Overleaf:* Snow threatens the Middletown Valley. As the sky darkens, horses are led into the barn, and a light from the farmhouse beckons: warmth, supper, family, and friends.

Left: Glimpsed from a thousand feet in the air, these ancient Allegheny Mountains west of Cumberland cast a series of spear-shaped shadows. *Right:* All Maryland lakes are man-made, and Garrett County's Deep Creek Lake is the largest. Created in 1923 as a hydro-electric project, it has long been a favorite recreational site for water sports and today draws visitors from many states. Boaters make one last run during the waning moments of another perfect day.

AFTERWORD

Maryland — we always had to drive through Maryland. I was born and raised near Philadelphia, but since my family spent every grade and high school summer in North Carolina, we always drove through Maryland, the first landmark on the trip south and the last on the return home.

After my military service, I moved to Washington, D.C., to work for the *National Geographic* and settled nearby in Maryland. But when I returned to Pennsylvania to visit family and friends, I still drove through Maryland. For me Maryland was the Beltway, I-95, the Baltimore Tunnel, and still more I-95. So when the opportunity came three years ago to begin this book, I was excited about exploring what had become my own backyard and for the chance to *really* drive through Maryland.

Now that 35,000 miles of Maryland have passed beneath my camper, I wish I'd started sooner to discover my own backyard and the people who live here. Of all the people I've encountered in my professional assignments throughout the world, residents of Maryland have been the most friendly and the most helpful. I wish I could cross paths with and thank again the many hundreds of Marylanders I met during my exploration.

The people whose assistance during this project I very much appreciate number well over two hundred, and I cannot thank each of you in print. To the following individuals I am deeply indebted: Dewitt Jones, for years of friendship and guidance, and the introduction which led to this project; Mianna Jopp and Lester Trott, of the Maryland State Tourism Department, for their indefatigable assistance and unending knowledge; Dave Harp, Bob Madden, Otis Imboden, and Eric Poggenpohl, for freely sharing their years of Maryland photographic experience and expertise; Jim Sugar, for his superb abilities as a pilot; and Bill and Lucy Garrett, Gil Grosvenor, Bob and Jan Gilka, and Joyce Graves of the *National Geographic,* for their years of inspiration and guidance.

Although there is room for only one person behind the camera, the love, support, and encouragement of the following people made me feel I was never alone: Barbara, Malan and Hank Strong, Ken and Lucie Garrett, Bill and Prisca Weems, Dick and Bonnie Durrance, Paddy Currie, Caren Keshishian, Catherine Wrather, and Greta Rosenzweig.

My greatest appreciation is for the love and understanding of my family: Mom, Dad, Sarah, John, Alison, Susan, Annie, and Ray. This book is dedicated to them.

—Steve Uzzell